GARFIELD GOES HOLLYWOOD

BY: JIM DAVIS

BALLANTINE BOOKS • NEW YORK

D0517200

Copyright © 1987 by United Feature Syndicate, Inc.

GARFIELD GOES HOLLYWOOD is based on the television special written by
Jim Davis, directed by Phil Roman, in association with United Media-Mendelson
Productions © 1987 United Feature Syndicate, Inc.

All rights reserved under International and Pan-American Copyright Conventions.
Published in the United States by Ballantine Books, a division of Random House,
Inc., New York, and simultaneously in Canada by Random House of Canada
Limited, Toronto.

Library of Congress Catalog Card Number: 87-91123

ISBN: 0-345-34580-0

Manufactured in the United States of America

First Edition: April 1987

10   9   8   7   6   5   4

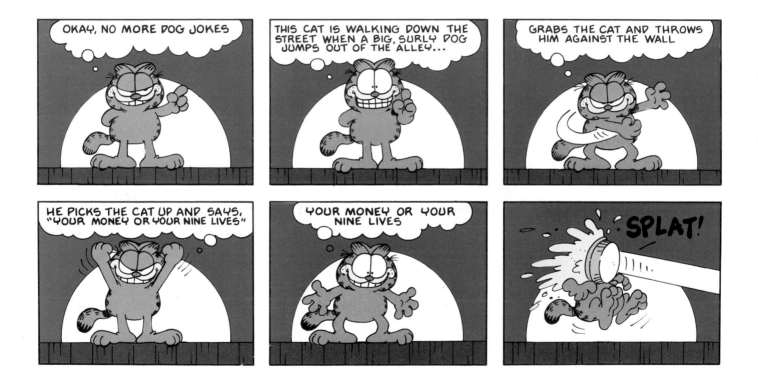

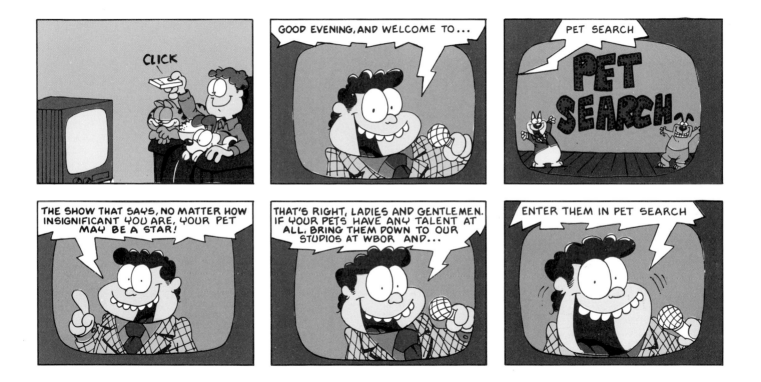

SPLOOSH

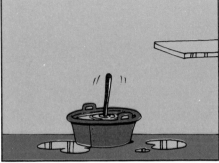

AAAAAAAAACCK!

SPLOOSH!

SPLOOSH!

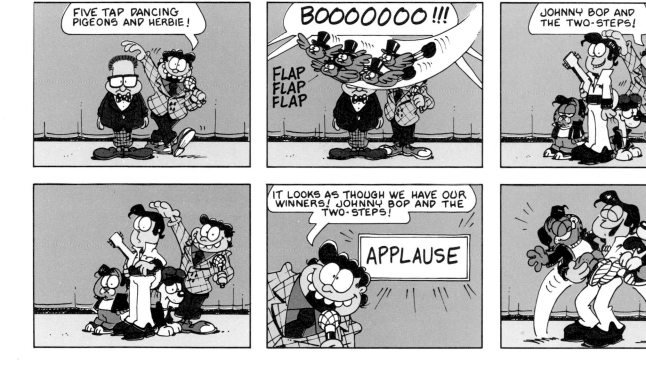

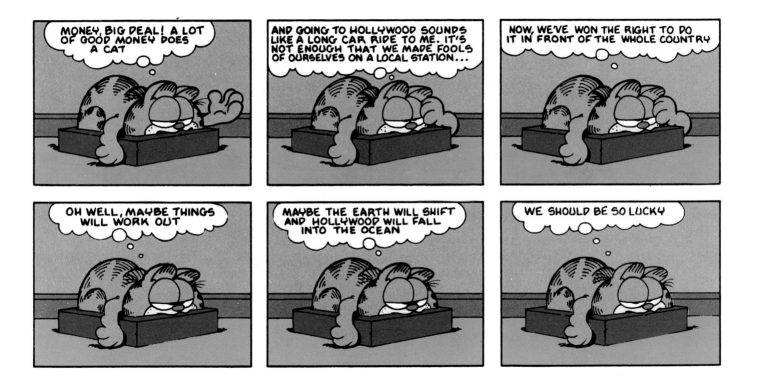

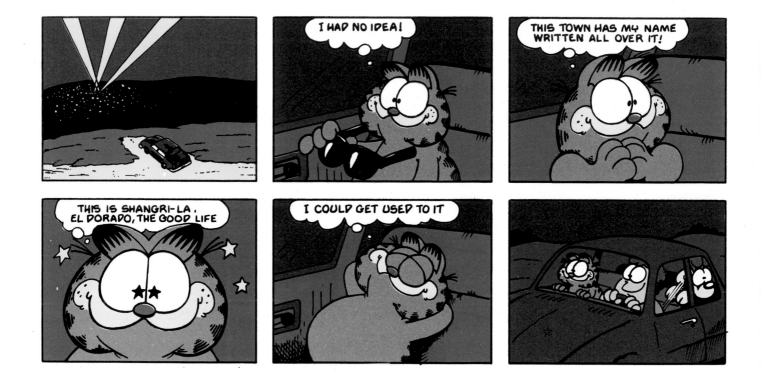

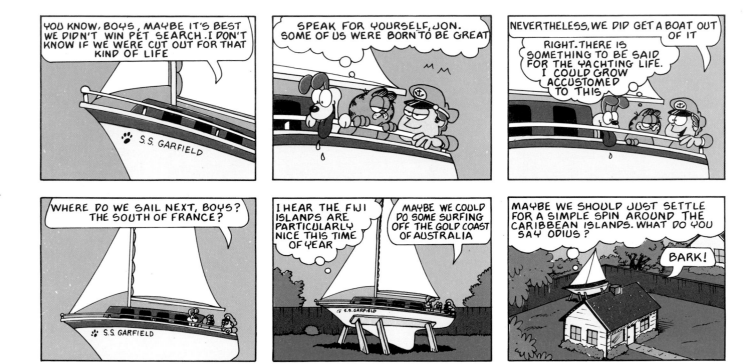

STRIPS, SPECIALS OR BESTSELLING BOOKS...
GARFIELD'S ON EVERYONE'S MENU

Don't miss even one episode in the Tubby Tabby's hilarious series!

__GARFIELD AT LARGE (#1)   32013-1/$5.95
__GARFIELD GAINS WEIGHT (#2)   32008-5/$5.95
__GARFIELD BIGGER THAN LIFE (#3)   32007-7/$5.95
__GARFIELD WEIGHS IN (#4)   32010-7/$5.95
__GARFIELD TAKES THE CAKE (#5)   32009-3/$5.95
__GARFIELD EATS HIS HEART OUT (#6)   32018-2/$5.95
__GARFIELD SITS AROUND THE HOUSE (#7)   32011-5/$5.95
__GARFIELD TIPS THE SCALES (#8)   33580-5/$5.95
__GARFIELD LOSES HIS FEET (#9)   31805-6/$5.95
__GARFIELD MAKES IT BIG (#10)   31928-1/$5.95
__GARFIELD ROLLS ON (#11)   32634-2/$5.95
__GARFIELD OUT TO LUNCH (#12)   33118-4/$5.95
__GARFIELD FOOD FOR THOUGHT (#13)   34129-5/$5.95

TV SPECIALS
__HERE COMES GARFIELD (#1)   32012-3/$5.95
__GARFIELD ON THE TOWN (#2)   31542-2/$4.95
__GARFIELD IN THE ROUGH (#3)   32242-8/$5.95
__GARFIELD IN DISGUISE (#4)   33045-5/$5.95
__GARFIELD IN PARADISE (#5)   33796-4/$5.95
__GARFIELD GOES HOLLYWOOD (#6)   34580-0/$5.95

GARFIELD AT HIS SUNDAY BEST!
__GARFIELD TREASURY   32106-5/$8.95
__THE SECOND GARFIELD TREASURY   33276-8/$8.95
__THE THIRD GARFIELD TREASURY   32635-0/$8.95

GARFIELD SPECIALS
__GARFIELD: HIS 9 LIVES   32061-1/$8.95
__THE UNABRIDGED, UNCENSORED, UNBELIEVABLE
   GARFIELD   33772-7/$5.95
__THE GARFIELD TRIVIA BOOK   33771-9/$5.95

BB BALLANTINE MAIL SALES
Dept. TA, 201 E. 50th St., New York, N.Y. 10022

Please send me the BALLANTINE or DEL REY BOOKS I have checked above.
I am enclosing $. . . . . (add .75 per copy to cover postage and
handling). Send check or money order — no cash or C.O.D.'s please. Prices
and numbers are subject to change without notice.

Name_____

Address_____

City_____State_____Zip Code_____

Allow at least 4 weeks for delivery.

30   TA-135